Did You Know?

BRA

A

G000128575

Compiled by Julia Skinner

With particular reference to the work of Clive Hardy

THE FRANCIS FRITH COLLECTION

www.francisfrith.com

Based on a book first published in the United Kingdom in 2006 by The Francis Frith Collection®

This edition published exclusively for Identity Books in 2009 ISBN 978-1-84589-395-8

British Library Cataloguing in Publication Data

Did You Know? Bradford - A Miscellany
Compiled by Julia Skinner
With particular reference to the work of Clive Hardy

The Francis Frith Collection
Frith's Barn, Teffont,
Salisbury, Wiltshire SP3 5QP
Tel: +44 (0) 1722 716 376
Email: info@francisfrith.co.uk
www.francisfrith.com

Printed and bound in Singapore

Front Cover: **BRADFORD, FORSTER SQUARE 1897** 39506p

The colour-tinting is for illustrative purposes only, and is not intended to be historically accurate

CONTENTS

INTRODUCTION

In the 19th century Bradford was the centre of the woollen and worsted industry, not only in Britain but also throughout the world. The Victorian traveller would have found the city skyline a veritable forest of mill chimneys, but there were also other industries. Bradford was on the edge of the great Yorkshire coalfield, and because the coal was near to the surface, it could be mined relatively inexpensively. Also close by were the ironworks of Bowling and Low Moor.

Just when Bradford's association with the woollen industry began is unknown, however it seems that some weaving was carried on in the area in the late 13th century. The woollen industry throughout Yorkshire was greatly influenced by the activities of the great Cistercian monasteries, and the abbey most closely associated with Bradford was Kirkstall, which was given lands around Bradford and the charter to hold Wibsey Fair.

Towards the latter part of the 17th century the spinning of worsted yarn gained a foothold around Halifax and Bradford, and by the late 18th century Yorkshire had replaced East Anglia as the country's leading manufacturer of worsted. The prospect of work in the new factories attracted thousands of people from rural areas to Bradford, but their new working conditions would probably have been very different to what they had been used to: strict discipline, regular attendance, long hours and unsafe working practices contrasted with the farm work or cottage-industry conditions that many people had worked in before. Living conditions were often appalling, and families were often crowded into a single room or cellars. Sanitation in most cases was merely a cesspit, which contaminated the water supply. Public health measures for the new industrial cities were not taken until after several outbreaks of cholera resulted in thousands of deaths nationwide.

A large manufacturing base grew up in Bradford to support the textile mills and machinery; this led to a profitable diversification, with a wide variety of industries thriving in the city. Most of the older

textile mills and some of the heavier industries have now closed down, but Bradford remains one of the most important cities in the north of England, with modern engineering, chemicals and financial services being important to the local economy.

Bradford has attracted immigrants for hundred of years, and 21st-century Bradford is a city with a rich cultural diversity. Peel Park is the venue for the annual Mela, a celebration of eastern culture, and Bradford is nationally famous for its ethnic restaurants, where some of Britain's finest Anglo-Asian cuisine can be enjoyed.

Today Bradford is a city where there are exciting plans for the future, with much investment planned for regeneration, but with the legacy of its industrial past still evident in wonderful - and valued - buildings and architecture. The story of this historic and important city is full of fascinating characters and events, of which this book can only provide a brief glimpse.

FORSTER SQUARE c1950 B173027

LOCAL DIALECT WORDS AND PHRASES

'Tyke' - the broad Yorkshire dialect.

'Put 't wood in 't 'oil!' - close the door!

'Shuck' - crazy'.

'Gerrod o' thissen' - sort yourself out, get a grip.

'E's double fisted an' threpple thrioted' - someone who is both aggressive and a heavy drinker (double fisted and triple throated).

'A brussen tup' - someone who is full of his own importance.

'Ginnel' - an alley or narrow passageway.

'Ippens' - nappies.

'Bairn' - a baby.

'Featherlegged' - very tired.

'Sackless' - lazy.

'Bahn' - to go somewhere.

'Muckment' - rubbish, refuse.

HAUNTED BRADFORD

One of the most famous ghost stories associated with Bradford comes from the time of the Civil War, when the town was being besieged by the Royalist forces of the Earl of Newcastle. During the siege the earl stayed at Bolling Hall, which was then outside the town and was the home of the Royalist Sir Richard Tempest. The story goes that the earl was so enraged by the continued resistance of the people of Bradford that one night he went to bed declaring that when the town was taken, he would slaughter every man, woman and child in the place. He was woken during the night by the sensation of the bedclothes being pulled away, and opened his eyes to the sight of a ghost standing beside him, wringing its hands and moaning 'Pity poor Bradford!'. The experience shook the earl so much that he changed his plans, deciding that he would only attack those who resisted him. Bradford eventually fell to the earl, who appears to have kept his word.

The famous 19th-century actor Sir Henry Irving died in Bradford in 1905 after suffering a stroke onstage whilst performing at the Bradford Theatre. He was taken to the Midland Hotel where he died soon after. Although he was buried in Westminster Abbey, his ghost is said to haunt the Bradford hotel where he breathed his last.

Jim Craven Well in the village of Thornton, a few miles from Bradford, was once believed to be the haunt of the ghost of 'Peggy wi't lantern', and also a giant dog with red eyes and a huge tail that was known as 'Bloody Tongue'.

BRADFORD MISCELLANY

Recorded on a tomb in a cemetery in Bradford:
'Here lies my poor wife, without bed or blanket.
But dead as a door nail. God by thankit.'

In recent years hundreds of carved stone heads have come to light in the West Riding, particularly in the Bradford area, which have become known as the Bradford Heads. Some may date from the Iron Age period, but others appear to only be around 100 years old. It is known that Iron Age people put the severed heads of their enemies, or possibly their replicas in stone, as guardians over the entrances of buildings and farmsteads. It seems that in the Bradford area the custom of putting stone heads in the drystone walls of fields and above cottage doors continued well into the 19th century.

The first written account of Bradford comes from the Domesday Book of 1086, William the Conqueror's great survey of his new lands. The entry covers the village itself together with several outlying hamlets and a number of manors. The total population was almost certainly less than 1,000 people, of which about 200 would be living in the village. The biggest landowner in the area was a man named Gamel. Of Norse descent, Gamel farmed a number of plots throughout the area.

THE SALT MONUMENT
1888 21011

MILL WORKERS F6039

Hand-weaving was considered a man's job in the old cottage industry system. Power looms did not make much of an impression in Bradford factories until the 1830s, but once their advantages were seen they soon took over, enabling women and girls to weave. 'The low price of female labour makes it the most profitable as well as the most agreeable for a female … Mr E., a manufacturer, employs females exclusively … with a decided preference to married females, especially those who have families at home dependent on them for support; they are attentive, docile, more so than unmarried females, and are compelled to use their utmost exertions to procure the necessities of life'.

From a Factory Commissioners' report on working conditions, in Ivy Pinchbeck's 'Women Workers and the Industrial Revolution 1750-1850', (1930).

Bradford is in the old West Riding of Yorkshire, which originally extended down to Sheffield. It was Viking Danes who first divided the huge county of Yorkshire into the ridings, or 'thridings' - thirds - and they became the North, East and West Ridings before local government reorganisation in 1974.

Mechanisation was viewed with suspicion by many workers in the cloth industry, who feared for their jobs. The fear manifested itself in Luddism; the Luddites fought against technical innovation, and mills were attacked, machinery was destroyed and manufacturers were threatened. In 1822 a power loom was smuggled into a mill in Shipley, but word got out and the place was soon surrounded by angry weavers. The loom was dismantled and taken away, but the cart on which it was being carried was attacked.

SHIPLEY, MARKET PLACE 1909 61865

THE TOWN HALL 1888 21007

In December 1642, during the Civil War, the Earl of Newcastle approached Bradford with a Royalist force. The town had declared for Parliament, and the parish church of St Peter's was fortified. The tower was protected from cannon shot with sheets of wool, and it was here that the citizens made their stand. The Royalists eventually captured the town, and an eye witness, Joseph Lister, recorded what Bradford was like after their forces left: he 'found few people left, but most of them scattered and fled away. I lodged in a cellar that night, but oh what a change was made in the town … nothing was left to eat or drink, or lodge upon, the streets being full of chaff and feathers, and meal, the enemies having emptied all the town of what was worth carrying away, and were now encamped near Bowling hall, and there kept fair and sold the things that would sell'.

Living conditions in industrial Bradford in the mid 19th century were appalling. Between 1801 and 1851 the population of Bradford grew from 13,000 to 104,000. Over 200 factory chimneys continually churned out black, sulphurous smoke, and Bradford gained the reputation of being the most polluted town in England. Sewage was dumped into the River Beck, and as people also obtained their drinking water from the river, this created serious health problems. Not surprisingly, there were regular outbreaks of cholera and typhoid. Only 30% of children born to textile workers lived to reach the age of fifteen, and it has been estimated that life expectancy in Bradford in the early 19th century was just over eighteen years, one of the lowest rates in the country.

PEEL PARK 1897 39529

In the 18th century the spinning of worsted yarn and the manufacture of worsted cloth became major industries in Bradford, thanks to men like John Hustler. Hustler, born in 1714, became a master manufacturer and merchant, and later served on the Worsted Committee, a body set up by the manufacturers to regulate and police the industry in an attempt to combat mounting fraud and theft among suppliers and outworkers. The Worsted Acts of 1777 allowed for the establishment of an inspectorate whose job it was to investigate possible cases of fraud and, if necessary, bring the transgressors to court. Hustler had been involved with a combination of manufacturers between 1754 and 1776, and it was this experience that led to his being appointed chairman of the Yorkshire committee. By 1773, such was the importance of worsted to Bradford that local manufacturers clubbed together to pay for a Piece Hall specialising in the sale of this type of cloth.

On the right of photograph 39506, below, is a statue of Richard Oastler in its original position in Forster Square. Richard Oastler fought against the use of child labour in the industrial mills. Yorkshire mill owners were at the forefront when it came to employing child labour in the 18th and 19th centuries. Many of these children were sent north from London workhouses. In the early days of the industrial revolution, those who ended up in the mills around Leeds were luckier than the children sent to Bradford: in Leeds they only had to work a 12-hour day, against a 13-hour day in Bradford, but in both places the children were beaten to keep them awake. Even children as young as five were sometimes expected to work these long hours. The statue of 'the Factory King' was later considered a traffic nuisance and was moved to Rawson Square; in recent years it was moved again to its present site on North Parade.

FORSTER SQUARE 1897 39506

The foundation stone for the Wool Exchange was laid by Lord Palmerston in 1864 (see photograph 39512 opposite). This proud trade house in the Venetian Gothic style was home to 3,000 dealers, with buyers and sellers trading wool from West Yorkshire, the Colonies and the Far East. It was said that whatever the type of wool or hair, a buyer would be found at the Bradford Exchange, and that when traders were about their buying and selling on Mondays and Thursdays, the place had the atmosphere of a madhouse. The Wool Exchange has now been sympathetically restored and the ground floor is used by the Waterstone's bookshop.

One of Bradford's prominent businessmen in the 19th century was Samuel Cunliffe Lister (after whom Lister Park was named), who came from a mill and quarry-owing family. Samuel gave up the manufacturing side of the business for a while to concentrate on woolcombing and the development of industry for the worsted trade. He went into partnership with George Donnisthorpe, a mechanic from Leeds, who had developed a woolcombing machine. Samuel knew that George's designs could be improved upon, and in 1843 they produced their first samples of fine-combed Botany wool. They bought up most of the patents for combing machines, and put theirs on the market. With profits of £1,000 per machine, Lister became a very wealthy man, able to finance the building of his magnificent Manningham Mill. An enormous worsted and silk mill, Manningham had a total floor space of 26 acres. Its chimney, styled as an Italian campanula, is 255ft high and is known as Lister's pride - local tradition says that it can be seen from anywhere in Bradford.

Did You Know?
BRADFORD
A MISCELLANY

THE MECHANICS' INSTITUTE 1897 39514

Photograph 39514, above, shows the Mechanics' Institute at the corner of Market Street, which was built by Andrews and Pepper in 1871. In common with many of Bradford's Victorian public buildings, it is in the Italianate style, unfussy and restrained. Mechanics' Institutes were found in most industrial towns in the 19th century, and gave workers the chance to improve their educational and employment prospects: they offered educational courses, backed up with examinations, as well as evening classes and lectures.

In 'The Waste Land' (1922), T S Eliot describes a character as someone
' ... on whom assurance sits
As a silk hat on a Bradford millionaire'.

Bradford's first public park was Peel Park, opened in 1863 and named in honour of Sir Robert Peel, advocate of Free Trade, who had been instrumental in the abolition of the unpopular Corn Laws.

Bradford was not served by a direct rail link until July 1846, when the Leeds & Bradford Railway opened for traffic. Four years later, the Lancashire & Yorkshire Railway reached the town, followed in 1854 by the Great Northern Railway. Bradford was never to be on a through route, though the Midlands Railway had planned to build a new line from Royston via the Spen Valley to link up with the Shipley-Bradford line. Some work was done, but the project was finally killed off with the outbreak of the First World War.

SALTAIRE, THE RAILWAY STATION 1909 61871

BRADFORD

A MISCELLANY

GREENGATES, THE LEEDS AND LIVERPOOL CANAL c1955 G115012

The 127-mile-long Leeds and Liverpool Canal was one of the great civil engineering projects of the 18th century, but in spite of Bradford's growing importance, the nearest the canal got to the town was at Shipley. It was not until 1820 that a three-mile-long canal from Shipley to the centre of Bradford was opened.

In May 1904, the people of Bradford turned out to welcome the Prince and Princess of Wales when they came to Lister Park to open the Bradford Exhibition, an inaugural display of art treasures and industrial machinery. The lake in the park was the venue for a number of naval battles using scaled-down models of warships.

The story of the days when Bradford was the woollen capital of the world is told at the Industrial and Horses at Work Museum, in a former spinning mill at Eccleshill. The attractions include working machinery, horse-drawn rides, textile workers' cottages, and the mill owner's house.

In the background of photograph 39509 below is the Venetian Gothic-style Wool Exchange, which was said to present an animated sight on Mondays and Thursdays when the traders did their buying and selling. This photograph also shows a policeman standing in the centre of the cobbled intersection. 200 years ago Bradford's 6,000 inhabitants were looked after by just two constables and a handful of deputies. There were also six night watchmen available, but they only patrolled property belonging to those willing to pay for the service.

MARKET STREET 1897 39509

LISTER PARK, THE GATEWAY
1897 39524

The imposing gateway in Lister Park seen in photograph 39524, opposite, is not as ancient as it appears. It was created in the Norman style - with battlemented roofs, towers and portcullis - using stonework which had previously formed part of the structure of the old Christ Church, which stood in Darley Street.

In 1904 Bradford City Council decided to provide free school meals for all local schoolchildren, a move initiated by Councillor Fred Jowett in response to the hunger and illness that the city's working-class schoolchildren were perceived to be suffering. By doing this, the city council was breaking the law of the time, which forbade such expenditure from local authority funds. Bradford City Council argued that if the law made it compulsory for parents to send children to school, then the council had an obligation to feed them whilst they were there. In 1906 Fred Jowett was elected Bradford's Member of Parliament, and was responsible for the implementation of an Education Act which empowered local authorities nationally to provide free school meals for those children in need.

In 1903 the world-famous Buffalo Bill brought his Wild West Show to Bradford. Buffalo Bill, whose real name was William Cody, had been a Pony Express rider, Civil War soldier, buffalo hunter, Army scout, and Indian fighter. After the west was won, he took his Wild West Show round America and Europe for many years. Nearly 28,000 people came to watch the two shows put on at Thornbury, although the tents were battered by gale force winds and heavy rain, where they saw 800 performers and 500 horses re-enact 'cowboy and indian' battles, including a chase after the Deadwood Stage. Sadly, the legendary sharp-shooter Annie Oakley did not appear in the shows at Bradford, having retired a few years earlier.

The important thoroughfare of Manningham Lane is seen in photograph 48570, opposite. The building on the left of the photograph, with its wrought-iron colonnaded front, is the Theatre Royal, where the famous actor Sir Henry Irving gave his final performance on 13 October 1905. After retiring to his hotel for the night he was taken ill, and died. The Theatre Royal was later used as a cinema, and was eventually demolished in 1976.

Titus Salt was one of the most influential men in the history of Bradford. He was apprenticed as a woolcomber, after which he joined his father Daniel's firm, taking it over when his father retired, and he eventually became the largest employer in Bradford. Titus's love affair with alpaca wool (from a llama-like South American animal) began when he spotted some unwanted bales in a warehouse. Taking a sample, he asked his father's opinion, and was advised to leave it well alone. Like most sons, Titus ignored his father's advice, bought the entire shipment and had it woven. The soft, light yet warm alpaca cloth soon caught on, and the Salts prospered. What set Titus Salt apart from many other Bradford mill workers was his concern for the welfare of the people who worked in his mill. His Victorian idealism led him to believe that a happy, healthy and fulfilled workforce was a productive workforce, and between 1850 and 1853 he built a state-of-the-art mill and a model industrial village for his workers which he called Saltaire; this was developed alongside a canal, river and railway, well away from the pollution of Bradford. Provision was made for welfare benefits and help was given to the aged, infirm and sick. When the village was completed there were 850 houses and 45 almshouses.

MANNINGHAM LANE 1902 48570

SALTAIRE, THE MILL AND THE CRICKET PITCH 1888 21024

A JOWETT JAVELIN c1955 A161014x

The Industrial and Horses at Work Museum at Moorside Mills has several Jowett cars in its collection, made by Bradford's Jowett Car Company. This was founded in 1910 by Benjamin and William Jowett, who ran a cycle works in Bradford, and was famous for the Bradford van, and the Jowett Javelin and Jupiter cars. The company ceased production in 1954. A Jowett Javelin can be seen in photograph A161014x, above.

One of the few mill owners in Bradford in the mid 19th century who was concerned about the smoke produced by the industrial mills and factories was Titus Salt. He discovered that the Rodda Smoke Burner produced very little pollution, and in 1842 he had these placed in all his premises. He tried to persuade other local businessmen to do the same, but most of them did not accept that the smoke was dangerous to people's health. Titus Salt became mayor of Bradford in 1848, but his failure to persuade the council to pass a bylaw making Rodda Smoke Burners compulsory in all the Bradford mills and factories was one of the factors that prompted him to build his model factory and village of Saltaire, then three miles outside the town.

Clayton, situated to the west of the centre of Bradford, was the home of Albert Pierrepoint (1905-1992), the most famous member of a Yorkshire family which provided three of Britain's Chief Executioners - the other two members were his father and uncle. Albert Pierrepoint was in office between 1932 and 1956, and is believed to have executed 433 men and 17 women; this total includes some 200 Nazis who were executed for war crimes after the Second World War. However, Pierrepoint's experiences made him an opponent of capital punishment, which was effectively abolished in the United Kingdom in 1965. He observed that most of his 'clients' were sentenced for crimes which had been committed in the heat of the moment rather than as premeditated acts, and that hanging could never be a deterrent to such actions. In his autobiography, 'Executioner: Pierrepoint', he commented: 'I have come to the conclusion that executions solve nothing, and are only an antiquated relic of a primitive desire for revenge which takes the easy way and hands over the responsibility for revenge to other people ... The trouble with the death penalty has always been that nobody wanted it for everybody, but everybody differed about who should get off'. A film about his career, titled 'Pierrepoint', starring Timothy Spall, was released in 2006.

SALTAIRE, VICTORIA ROAD 1909 61869

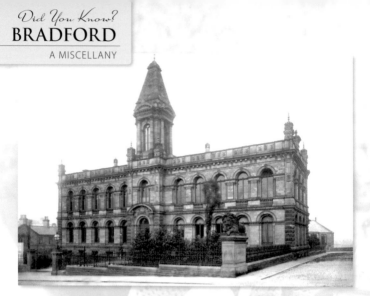

SALTAIRE, THE INSTITUTE 1893 33192

SALTAIRE, SALT'S MILL 1903 49705

The Club and Institute at Saltaire, now the Victoria Hall, provided enlightenment and education for the workers and their children. It contained a library, reading rooms, a gymnasium, a billiards room and a lecture hall for 800 people. There were two statues of lions outside the Institute and two more across the road outside the school, which were originally made for London's Trafalgar Square, but were considered too small (see photograph 33192, opposite).

Titus Salt's mill at Saltaire was the largest in Europe: the weaving shed housed 1,200 looms and a workforce in excess of 3,000. The first mill building was erected in 1853, and a second in 1865. Attempts were made to reduce noise in the mill by placing much of the shafting which drove the machinery underground, and good ventilation systems removed dust and dirt from the factory floor. The mill chimney was fitted with Rodda Smoke Burners, to make sure that the surrounding neighbourhood was not polluted with smoke. Increased competition from factories abroad finally forced the closure of the mill in 1986. Since then it has been given a new lease of life - it now incorporates several shops, three art galleries and industrial units for high-tech businesses.

As there were no public houses in Saltaire, many of Titus Salt's workers ventured into the neighbouring town of Shipley to visit the inns there. However, if they over-indulged and were brought up before the authorities for being drunk and disorderly they could expect no mercy - the teetotaller Titus Salt was one of Bradford's leading magistrates.

Titus Salt's model village of Saltaire provided all the essential living amenities, and for recreation he provided a spacious park on the opposite side of the river and canal. Here, splendid gardens, with statues of Salt, offered healthy recreation facilities to the workers at the giant mill. The park was later called Roberts Park, after being bought by another industrialist, and was then offered to Bradford Council.

SALTAIRE, ROBERTS PARK 1909 61872

The most popular museum in the United Kingdom outside London is in Bradford, and attracts around 800,000 visitors a year. The National Museum of Photography, Film and Television (NMPFT), founded in 1983, is part of the British National Museum of Science and Industry, and portrays the past, present and future of the media. The main attraction is the massive screen of the IMAX cinema, which gives the viewer an exceptionally dramatic film-going experience. The museum holds the first-ever photographic negative, and also the world's first example of moving pictures - a piece of film of Leeds Bridge, which dates from 1888.

The Titus Salt Monument is seen in photograph 21011, on page 7, in its original position outside the Town Hall. It was erected there in 1874, but was later moved to Lister Park because of traffic congestion. The seated figure of Sir Titus Salt is carved from white Italian marble, and shows him holding the plans of Saltaire in his left hand.

Titus Salt was obviously an enlightened man; as well as supporting adult suffrage and being a severe critic of the draconian 1834 New Poor Law, he also supported the move to reduce working hours and was the first employer in Bradford to introduce a working day limited to 10 hours. However there are some interesting contradictions in his views: he refused to allow his workforce to join trade unions, and, most strange of all, he was totally opposed to legislation restricting child labour. Salt was happy to employ children in his factories, and disagreed with the 1833 Factory Act which attempted to make it illegal to employ children under the age of nine in textile mills

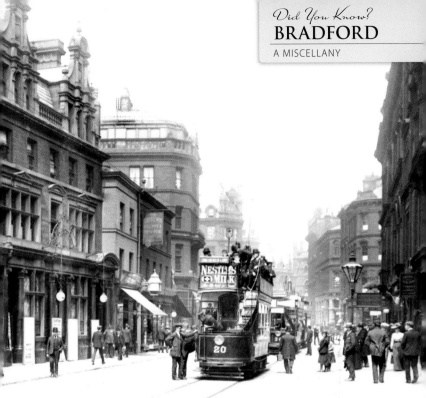

TYRRELL STREET 1903 49713

Electric street tramcars, such as those seen in photograph 49713, above, were first introduced into Bradford in 1892, when a 36-seater, double-decker tramcar was demonstrated on 660 yards of track from Forster Square up Cheapside to Manor Row; however, it was to be another six years before Corporation electric trams were put into service. The first route ran to Bolton, later extended to Eccleshill and Thackley. Once established, electric tramcars ran in Bradford until 1950, although they were in competition against trolleybuses from 1928.

Did You Know?
BRADFORD
A MISCELLANY

THE INFIRMARY 1897 39522

Bradford was a pioneering town in matters of public health; it established one of the very earliest municipal hospitals in Britain, as well as separate medical and dental services for schools. During ward rounds, patients at the town infirmary had to stay still and lie at attention in their beds, and were instructed not to speak to the doctor or the matron unless they were asked a specific question.

In 1882 Bradford's Technical College became independent from the Mechanics' Institute and was given its own premises, seen in photograph 23495, opposite. The people of Bradford saw the college as essential to their efforts to keep abreast of the competition from France in the production of quality woollen cloths.

The three literary Brontë sisters, Charlotte, Emily, and Anne, were born in Thornton on the outskirts of Bradford. The Brontë family later moved to the village of Haworth, a small town of cobbled streets and plain grey houses set amidst the Yorkshire moors near Keighley, about ten miles north-east of Bradford, where their father Patrick was vicar of the Church of St Michael and All Angels. The landscape around Haworth is beautiful but bleak, and the sisters led solitary lives; their surroundings gave them the inspiration for their novels, the most famous of which are 'Jane Eyre', 'Wuthering Heights' and 'The Tenant of Wildfell Hall'.

THE TECHNICAL COLLEGE 1890 23495

FORSTER SQUARE 1903 49711

THE CARTWRIGHT MEMORIAL HALL c1950 B173024

Forster Square was named after the Bradford Member of Parliament W E Forster, who sponsored the Compulsory Education Act of 1870. A statue of Forster, 'the Education King', can be seen in photograph 49711, opposite. It was thanks to people like Forster and Fred Jowett (see page 21) that Bradford was the first place in the country to have school medical services, school meals, a school board, school baths and nursery provision. On the right of the photograph the solid and monumental warehouses of the Bradford Dyer's Association can be seen, which were built in the mid 1860s. The area around here is known as 'Little Germany' owing to the large numbers of Germans who colonised Bradford in the Victorian era and established warehouses.

The land at Manningham which now forms Lister Park was purchased by the Corporation at a knock-down price in 1870. It was originally the ancestral home and estate of Samuel Cunliffe Lister, who was afterwards created Baron Masham (see page 14). Lister's old mansion was demolished by the Corporation and following a substantial donation of £47,000, the Libraries and Art Gallery Committee erected the Cartwright Memorial Hall on the site in 1904. The building now houses one of the city's best museums and art galleries. It holds important collections of 19th- and early 20th-century paintings, including work by Gainsborough, Reynolds and Stanley Spencer, and many by the Pre-Raphaelite Brotherhood. More recent acquisitions include work by Bradford's own David Hockney.

VICTORIA SQUARE c1950 B173028

Photograph B173028, above, shows Victoria Square just before the abandonment of the tramway system in May 1950. In the background a trolleybus is about to pass a tram as it heads towards the Town Hall. Like the electric tramcar, the trolleybus drew its power from overhead, but unlike the tramcar it did not require rails. Bradford was not only the first place in the country to introduce trolleybuses, but also the last to discontinue their service - the system survived until 1972.

Bradford's cathedral - formerly St Peter's Church - nestles on a hillside above Forster Square, its sturdy tower peeping above the roofs. The church was built in the Perpendicular style in millstone grit; the nave and chancel were erected in 1458, and the tower half a century later. Although cathedral status had been granted to St Peter's in 1919, work on upgrading and extending the building did not begin until the 1950s. Among the improvements were a new chancel, a song room and a vestry for the bishop.

Bradford's trade unionists played an important part in British political history. In 1891 Bradford experienced a strike by the mill workers which lasted almost five months; the reason was an imposed reduction in wages at Lister's Mills due to a fall-off in orders. A meeting at St George's Hall ended with strikers clashing with police. The following night it is said that 20,000 people rioted, and troops were called in to assist the civil powers. On the third night a searchlight was mounted on the tower of the Town Hall, and troops were again called in; there were a number of baton charges and arrests before the mob was finally dispersed. The strikers returned to work having gained nothing, but a direct result of the Lister's strike was the founding of the Independent Labour Party at a conference held in Bradford in 1893. Among those present were Keir Hardie (who went on to become the first Labour Member of Parliament), the Socialist writer George Bernard Shaw, and Fred Jowett, who was elected Member of Parliament for Bradford in 1906 (and see page 21).

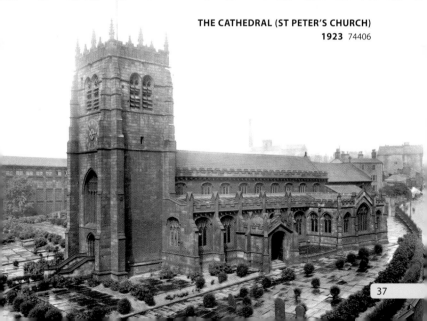

THE CATHEDRAL (ST PETER'S CHURCH)
1923 74406

Bradford's splendid and distinctive Gothic Town Hall with its 200ft tower, modelled on the Palazzo Vecchio in Florence, was completed in 1873 at a cost of £100,000. It was designed by the local architects Lockwood and Mawson to rival the new town halls of neighbouring Leeds and Halifax. By the time that photograph 49712, opposite, was taken, it was clearly showing the effects of 30 years of exposure to industrial pollution. The building was given a thorough clean in the early 1970s. The name of the Town Hall was changed to the City Hall in 1965, rather belatedly as Bradford achieved city status in 1897!

Anthrax has hit the headlines in recent years as a possible weapon of biological warfare or terrorist attacks, but in the 19th century all workers who handled wool or animal hair and hides were at risk of catching this swift-acting and deadly disease. These products were such an important part of Bradford's trade and industry, and the disease became so prevalent amongst its workers, that anthrax at one time was known as the Bradford Disease. In the 1890s Bradford and District Trade and Labour Council appointed Frederick William Eurich to work in a pathological and bacteriological laboratory in the city, in a small room in the Technical College. Eurich's parents had come to Bradford from Germany when he was a small boy, in search of work; when he grew up Eurich trained as a physician, and his work in Bradford eventually led to the conquest of anthrax. After years of experiments which put himself in considerable danger, Eurich came to realise that the disease was transferred to humans when they came into contact with blood from an infected animal. The use of formaldehyde and rigorous precautions and inspection of wool and other fibres led to a decrease in cases of anthrax, and in later years the development of antibiotics provided a cure for the disease. Eurich, who retired in 1937, was awarded the Gold Medal of the Textile Institute in recognition of the thousands of lives in the textile industry that were saved as a result of his work.

LISTER PARK LAKE 1921 71629

THE TOWN HALL AND THE SQUARE 1903 49712

THE CHILDREN'S HOSPITAL 1897 39523

HORTON PARK BRIDGE 1897 39531

Throughout much of the 19th century, Bradford's death rate among children under five years of age was a disgrace. In 1876 alone, over 2,000 of Bradford's under-fives died. The imposing building seen in 39523, opposite, its sparse decoration bringing it a somewhat severe appearance, was one of several charitable concerns in Bradford which were founded in the later years of the century, when there was a more enlightened attitude to public health and welfare. As well as an Infirmary there was an Eye and Ear Hospital, a Blind Institution, a Fever Hospital and orphanages for both boys and girls.

One of Bradford's famous literary sons was the author and playwright J B Priestley, who was born in Mannheim Road, Bradford, on 13 September 1894. His father was a teacher at Belle Vue Boys' School, where Priestley later received his schooling. After leaving school in 1910 he began work as a junior clerk with the wool merchants Helm & Co in the Swan Arcade in Market Street, but his dream was to write. After service in the First World War he began to write articles for the Yorkshire Observer, and his career took off. Although he later moved to London, he continued to visit the city regularly. His most famous work was his novel 'The Good Companions', published in 1929, which chronicles the adventures of Jess Oakroyd after leaving the mill town of 'Bruddersford', and the Dinky Doos concert party that he joins. The book was reviewed by the Bradford Daily Telegraph, which reported that: 'The reader is inevitably reminded of another writer who loved public houses and wayside encounters with anybody and everybody - Dickens, of course. Mr Priestley has the same gusto, the same zestful appreciation of their comic qualities. He invests his worst characters in a glamour which obscures their baser characteristics, and presents them mainly as figures of fun'. The book was a huge success; Bradford Public Library held 120 copies, but there were long waiting lists for the book, which broke all library records. J B Priestley was involved in the founding of the Bradford Civic Theatre, and is now commemorated in its new name of The Priestley Centre for the Arts.

LISTER PARK, THE BANDSTAND 1923 74400

Lister's Mills at Manningham was once the world's biggest silk factory, providing silks and velvets for bus and train seats, humble houses and international palaces, including the White House in the USA. During the Second World War production was altered to help the war effort, and Lister's Mills made parachute silk and cord, and 50 miles of khaki cloth. But by 1992 the glory days of the mills were over, and the buildings were becoming derelict. The whole complex was bought by the regeneration organisation Urban Splash in 2000, and has now been repaired and turned into apartments and business space. One of the companies who will be working from the Lister's Mills complex will be the Bradford-based theatre company Mind The Gap, which is well-known nationally for its work with learning-disabled artists. The theatre company has been awarded nearly £1 million to create a landmark 'creation centre' at Lister's Mill, working in partnership with other arts organisations. The centre is due to open in the spring of 2007.

The Bradford author J B Priestley provided Britain with a rather strange morale-boosting symbol during the Second World War - a meat and potato pie. The pie which inspired Priestley had been a feature in the window of Arthur Roberts's food shop in Godwin Street for around 40 years; it actually consisted of a pie crust over an empty pie dish, which concealed a mechanism that puffed steam out of holes in the crust at intervals. During the war, Priestley broadcast a series of radio talks on Sunday evenings, and one day he visited Bradford just after the window of Arthur Roberts's shop had been blown off in an air raid. Priestley happened to wander past the shop, and there, in the partly boarded-up window, was the pie, still puffing away and trying to entice shoppers to come in and buy. Priestley described the scene in his radio broadcast: 'a giant, almost superhuman meat pie, with a magnificent brown, crisp, artfully wrinkled, succulent-looking crust … giving off a fine, rich, appetising steam to make your mouth water … a perpetual volcano of meat and potato … every puff defying Hitler, Goering and the whole gang of them'. It became one of Priestley's best-known broadcasts, much to the annoyance of Mr Roberts, who soon grew tired of the crowds of people who came to see the famous, bravely defiant pie.

THE WAR MEMORIAL 1923 74404

Did You Know?
BRADFORD
A MISCELLANY

FORSTER SQUARE c1950 B173027

SPORTING BRADFORD

Bradford Northern Rugby League Club was the first club after the Second World War to reach three successive Wembley Challenge Cup finals - in 1947, 1948 and 1949. Odsal Stadium, home of Bradford Northern Rugby League Club, for many years held the world record for attendance at a Rugby League match. 102,569 people officially attended the Challenge Cup Final replay between Halifax and Warrington in May 1954, although it was thought by many observers that the actual attendance was over 120,000. The record stood for over 40 years.

A Bradford boxer once fought Muhammad Ali for the world heavyweight title. He is Richard Dunn, who fought Ali in 1976. He earned the right to fight Ali after becoming the first man since Henry Cooper to defend the British heavyweight title. Sadly 'The Greatest' was just too strong for Dunn, but the Bradford man did at least make it into the fifth round, a highly creditable performance.

Bradford Park Avenue FC lost only 6 games at home in 7 years from 1922 to 1929. The club once played in front of a crowd of 82,771 against Manchester United in 1949. Avenue's most famous old boy is probably Ron Greenwood who went on to manage West Ham and England with great distinction. Possibly Avenue's finest player was Len Shackleton, who scored 171 goals for the club before moving to Newcastle United. Albert Geldard, who holds the record as the youngest player ever to play League football, was 15 years and 158 days old when he made his debut for Bradford Park Avenue Football Club in 1929. He also represented England before his 20th birthday.

Bradford City AFC had an eventful and unique early history. Their origins were in Manningham Rugby League Club. In 1903 the club switched to association football, and without having played a game were invited to join the Football League. This was an attempt to introduce soccer into a rugby-dominated area. City were the first West Riding club in the League. By 1911 the club had completed an astonishing rise, reaching the first division and winning the FA Cup. Bradford City's unusual colours of claret and amber are certainly distinctive. In opinion polls the shirt has been voted both best and worst shirt. City scarves are popular with fans of the 'Harry Potter' books, as they are also the colours of Hogwarts' School. Coincidentally, Bradford City actually had a player called Harry Potter before the First World War!

QUIZ QUESTIONS

Answers on page 50.

1. Why was it said that the Bradford pawnshops were full of watches in 1851?

2. Bradford is famous for being a centre of the worsted trade, but what is worsted?

3. Bradford's City Hall is adorned at the second floor level with 35 statues of Kings and Queens of England and the United Kingdom - except for one person. Who is it?

4. The Cartwright Memorial Hall was designed to hold Bradford's art treasures, but who is it named after, and what was his contribution to Bradford?

5. Titus Salt's model village of Saltaire, built in the mid 19th century, was missing two facilities usually found in towns at that time - what were they?

6. Which famous composer was born in Bradford in 1862?

7. What is the link between Bradford and a white cat called Percy?

8. Here's a nostalgic one for those of a certain age - who are Jemima, Hamble, Humpty, Big Ted and Little Ted, and where in Bradford can you find them?

9. How did Bradford get its name?

10. Which Pop Idol is a Bradford boy?

RECIPE

YORKSHIRE CURD TARTS

Ingredients
For the pastry:
100g/4oz butter or margarine
225g/8oz plain flour
1 tablespoon caster sugar
Pinch of salt
1 egg yolk
1-2 tablespoons cold water

For the filling:
225g/8oz fresh curd or
cottage cheese, sieved
50g/2oz caster sugar
1 teaspoon grated lemon
rind
2 eggs, separated
2 tablespoons currants or
sultanas
1 tablespoon melted butter
Pinch of nutmeg

Make the pastry by rubbing the fat into the flour, adding the sugar, salt and egg yolk, and mixing well. Finally add the cold water to make a firm dough. Turn out on to a floured surface and knead well, then roll into a ball and chill for at least 30 minutes.

Preheat the oven to 220 degrees C/425 degrees F/Gas Mark 7.

Mix together all the remaining ingredients except the egg whites. Roll out the pastry. Either line 12 greased deep patty tins or a 20-22cm (8-9 inch) greased flan tin with the pastry, and lightly prick over the bottom with a fork. Beat the egg whites until stiff, and lightly fold into the cheese mixture. Divide the mixture between the patty tin cases, or spread over the large flan tin, and cook in a preheated oven for 10 minutes, then reduce the oven temperature to 180 degrees C/350 degrees F/Gas Mark 4, and continue cooking for a further 20-25 minutes or until the cheese mixture is set and golden.

RECIPE

YORKSHIRE FAT RASCALS

Ingredients

450g/1lb plain flour
225g/8oz butter
25g/1oz light soft brown
sugar

Pinch of salt
115g/4oz currants
A small quantity of milk and
water mixed

Rub the butter into the flour. Add the sugar, salt and currants and mix to a firm dough with a little mixed water and milk. Roll out to about 1cm (½ inch) thick, and cut into 6cm (2½ inch) rounds. Dust with a little caster sugar and bake at 180 degrees C/350 degrees F/Gas Mark 4 for about 20 minutes.

Did You Know?
BRADFORD
A MISCELLANY

QUIZ ANSWERS

1. The Great Exhibition of 1851 proved to be a great hit with the Bradford mill workers. The travel agent Thomas Cook would send his son from Derby to Bradford on a Friday with several trains of empty carriages. John Cook then toured the streets accompanied by a band and persuaded the workers to part with five shillings each for their train fares. It was said that the local pawnshops at this time were full of watches deposited by workers raising extra cash for spending money on their day out.

2. Worsted is the name of both a yarn, usually made from wool, and the cloth made from this yarn. The essential feature of a worsted yarn is straightness of fibre. Wool for this yarn is made into continuous, untwisted strands which are then blended to make the fibres lie parallel. These blended strands are then tightly twisted ('worsted'), and spun. Worsted cloth, also known in the past as 'stuff', is lightweight with a hard, smooth texture. Only long and fine-stapled wool is used to make worsted cloth, which differs from woollens as the crimp of the natural wool fibre is removed in the spinning process; the removal of this crimp makes worsted fabric cooler to wear than woollen cloth made by other processes.

3. One of the statues is of Oliver Cromwell. Although he ruled the country, it was as Lord Protector, not as King.

4. It was named in memory of Dr Edmund Cartwright, who invented the power loom that brought so much wealth to Bradford.

5. Only two things were missing from Titus Salt's model village of Saltaire - a pub (he was firmly against alcohol) and a pawnshop.

6. The composer Frederick Delius was born in Bradford on 29 January 1862. His parents had come to England from Bielefeld, in Germany, and his father Julius was a prosperous businessman in the wool industry. Delius, who learned to play both violin and piano proficiently before he reached his teens, attended Bradford Grammar School from 1874 to 1878.

7. The famous artist David Hockney was born in Bradford in 1937 and educated at Bradford Grammar School and Bradford College of Art, before moving to London to study at the Royal College of Art. In 1970 David Hockney painted the fashion designer Ossie Clark with his then wife, Celia Birtwell, and their white cat, Percy, in their Notting Hill home. This painting, titled 'Mr and Mrs Clark and Percy', has become one of the most popular works in the collection of the Tate Gallery, and in 2005 was voted one of the top ten favourite paintings in the United Kingdom. However, it appears that the cat may not actually be Percy - Celia Birtwell has admitted that she thinks the cat that posed for Hockney was actually another white cat owned by the couple, called Blanche.

8. Jemima, Hamble, Humpty, Big Ted and Little Ted were the stars of the BBC's children's programme 'Play School', which was broadcast from 1964 to 1988. The original toys used in the programme can now be seen in the National Museum of Photography, Film and Television (NMPFT) in Bradford.

9. Bradford's name is derived from a 'Broad Ford' at Church Bank by the site of what is now Bradford's cathedral. A settlement had begun to appear at this spot in Anglo-Saxon times.

10. The pop singer Gareth Gates, who was born in Bradford on 12 July 1984. He shot to fame when he came second in the 2002 television talent show 'Pop Idol'.

THE ALHAMBRA c1955 B173043

FRANCIS FRITH

PIONEER VICTORIAN PHOTOGRAPHER

Francis Frith, founder of the world-famous photographic archive, was a complex and multi-talented man. A devout Quaker and a highly successful Victorian businessman, he was philosophical by nature and pioneering in outlook. By 1855 he had already established a wholesale grocery business in Liverpool, and sold it for the astonishing sum of £200,000, which is the equivalent today of over £15,000,000. Now in his thirties, and captivated by the new science of photography, Frith set out on a series of pioneering journeys up the Nile and to the Near East.

INTRIGUE AND EXPLORATION

He was the first photographer to venture beyond the sixth cataract of the Nile. Africa was still the mysterious 'Dark Continent', and Stanley and Livingstone's historic meeting was a decade into the future. The conditions for picture taking confound belief. He laboured for hours in his wicker dark-room in the sweltering heat of the desert, while the volatile chemicals fizzed dangerously in their trays. Back in London he exhibited his photographs and was 'rapturously cheered' by members of the Royal Society. His reputation as a photographer was made overnight.

VENTURE OF A LIFE-TIME

By the 1870s the railways had threaded their way across the country, and Bank Holidays and half-day Saturdays had been made obligatory by Act of Parliament. All of a sudden the working man and his family were able to enjoy days out, take holidays, and see a little more of the world.

With typical business acumen, Francis Frith foresaw that these new tourists would enjoy having souvenirs to commemorate their days out. For the next thirty years he travelled the country by train and by pony and trap, producing fine photographs of seaside resorts and beauty spots that were keenly bought by millions of Victorians. These prints were painstakingly pasted into family albums and pored over during the dark nights of winter, rekindling precious memories of summer excursions. Frith's studio was soon supplying retail shops all over the country, and by 1890 F Frith & Co had become the greatest specialist photographic publishing company in the world, with over 2,000 sales outlets, and pioneered the picture postcard.

FRANCIS FRITH'S LEGACY

Francis Frith had died in 1898 at his villa in Cannes, his great project still growing. By 1970 the archive he created contained over a third of a million pictures showing 7,000 British towns and villages.

Frith's legacy to us today is of immense significance and value, for the magnificent archive of evocative photographs he created provides a unique record of change in the cities, towns and villages throughout Britain over a century and more. Frith and his fellow studio photographers revisited locations many times down the years to update their views, compiling for us an enthralling and colourful pageant of British life and character.

We are fortunate that Frith was dedicated to recording the minutiae of everyday life. For it is this sheer wealth of visual data, the painstaking chronicle of changes in dress, transport, street layouts, buildings, housing and landscape that captivates us so much today, offering us a powerful link with the past and with the lives of our ancestors.

Computers have now made it possible for Frith's many thousands of images to be accessed almost instantly. The archive offers every one of us an opportunity to examine the places where we and our families have lived and worked down the years. Its images, depicting our shared past, are now bringing pleasure and enlightenment to millions around the world a century and more after his death.

For further information visit: www.francisfrith.com

INTERIOR DECORATION

Frith's photographs can be seen framed and as giant wall murals in thousands of pubs, restaurants, hotels, banks, retail stores and other public buildings throughout Britain. These provide interesting and attractive décor, generating strong local interest and acting as a powerful reminder of gentler days in our increasingly busy and frenetic world.

FRITH PRODUCTS

All Frith photographs are available as prints and posters in a variety of different sizes and styles. In the UK we also offer a range of other gift and stationery products illustrated with Frith photographs, although many of these are not available for delivery outside the UK – see our web site for more information on the products available for delivery in your country.

THE INTERNET

Over 100,000 photographs of Britain can be viewed and purchased on the Frith web site. The web site also includes memories and reminiscences contributed by our customers, who have personal knowledge of localities and of the people and properties depicted in Frith photographs. If you wish to learn more about a specific town or village you may find these reminiscences fascinating to browse. Why not add your own comments if you think they would be of interest to others? See **www.francisfrith.com**

PLEASE HELP US BRING FRITH'S PHOTOGRAPHS TO LIFE

Our authors do their best to recount the history of the places they write about. They give insights into how particular towns and villages developed, they describe the architecture of streets and buildings, and they discuss the lives of famous people who lived there. But however knowledgeable our authors are, the story they tell is necessarily incomplete.

Frith's photographs are so much more than plain historical documents. They are living proofs of the flow of human life down the generations. They show real people at real moments in history; and each of those people is the son or daughter of someone, the brother or sister, aunt or uncle, grandfather or grandmother of someone else. All of them lived, worked and played in the streets depicted in Frith's photographs.

We would be grateful if you would give us your insights into the places shown in our photographs: the streets and buildings, the shops, businesses and industries. Post your memories of life in those streets on the Frith website: what it was like growing up there, who ran the local shop and what shopping was like years ago; if your workplace is shown tell us about your working day and what the building is used for now. Read other visitors' memories and reconnect with your shared local history and heritage. With your help more and more Frith photographs can be brought to life, and vital memories preserved for posterity, and for the benefit of historians in the future.

Wherever possible, we will try to include some of your comments in future editions of our books. Moreover, if you spot errors in dates, titles or other facts, please let us know, because our archive records are not always completely accurate—they rely on 140 years of human endeavour and hand-compiled records. You can email us using the contact form on the website.

Thank you!

For further information, trade, or author enquiries please contact us at the address below:

The Francis Frith Collection, Frith's Barn, Teffont, Salisbury, Wiltshire, England SP3 5QP.

Tel: +44 (0)1722 716 376 Fax: +44 (0)1722 716 881
e-mail: sales@francisfrith.co.uk **www.francisfrith.com**